D0045439

Moments
for
Each Other

Moments
for
Each Other

by
Robert Strand

New Leaf Press

First printing, August 1994
Second printing, March 1996

ISBN: 0-89221-266-7
Library of Congress: 93-87689

Cover photo by Plumlee Photography, Oak Grove, AR

All Scripture references are from the New International Version, unless otherwise noted.

Every effort has been made to locate the authors or originators of the
stories contained in this book. Most are the result of conversations
with pastors, while others were accumulated throughout the course
of a 30-year radio and television broadcasting career.

Presented to:

_____

Presented by:

_____

Date:

_____

Day 1
The First Valentine

The story of Valentine's Day begins in the third century with an oppressive Roman emperor and a humble Christian martyr. The emperor was Claudius II, the Christian was Valentinus. Claudius had ordered all Romans to worship 12 gods and he had also made it a crime punishable by death to associate with Christians or worship their God. Valentinus was dedicated to the ideals of Christ and not even the threat of death could keep him from practicing his beliefs. He was arrested and imprisoned.

During the last weeks of Valentinus' life a quite remarkable thing happened. The jailer, noting that Valentinus was a man of refinement and learning, asked if it would be possible for him to bring his daughter, Julia, for lessons, for teaching. Julia had been blind since birth and was a beautiful girl with a quick mind. Valentinus read to her stories of Rome's history . . . he described the world of nature to her . . . he taught her mathematics . . . and told her about God. She, for the first time, began to see the world through his eyes, trusted in his wisdom, and found a special comfort in his quiet strength.

"Valentinus, does God hear our prayers?" Julia asked one day.

"Yes, my child, He hears each one," he replied.

"Do you know what I pray for every morning and every night?

I pray that I might be able to see. I want so much to see everything you've told me about!"

"God does what is best for us if we will only believe in Him," Valentinus said.

"Oh, Valentine, I do believe," Julia said intensely. "I do!" She then knelt and grasped his hand. They sat quietly, she kneeling, he sitting, each praying. Suddenly there was a brilliant light in the prison cell! Radiant, Julia screamed, "Valentinus, I can see! I can see!"

On the eve of his death, Valentinus wrote a last note to Julia, urging her to continue her learning and encouraging her to stay close to God. He signed it, "From Your Valentine!"

His death sentence was carried out the next day, February 14, 270. He was buried at what is now the Church of Praxedes in Rome. Legend tells us that Julia herself planted a pink-blossomed almond tree near his grave. Today, the almond tree remains the symbol of abiding love and friendship. On the anniversary of his death, February 14, St. Valentine's Day, messages of affection, love, and devotion are exchanged.

Today's Quote: *They who love are but one step from heaven.* — James Russell Lowell

Today's Verse: And now these three remain: faith, hope, and love. But the greatest of these is love (1 Cor. 13:13).

Day 2
The Test

His name was Lt. John Blanchard, a soldier in basic training in Florida during WWII. One evening he wandered into the post library and found a book to read. The feminine handwriting in the margins intrigued him, so he turned to the front of the book and found the name of the previous owner . . . a Miss Hollis Maynell.

Blanchard did some research and found her address in New York. The following day he was shipped overseas. For 13 months the two corresponded by letter and began to open their hearts to each other. He asked for her picture, to which she refused by saying that if he really loved her it wouldn't matter what she looked like.

Finally the day came when they were to meet in Grand Central Station, New York City. She had instructed, "You'll recognize me by the red rose that I'll be wearing on my lapel."

Let's let the young soldier tell you what happened:

> A young woman was coming toward me, beautiful, trim, blonde, eyes were blue as flowers, and in her pale green suit she was like springtime come alive. I started toward her forgetting that she was not wearing the rose . . . and then I saw Hollis Maynell!
>
> She was standing behind the girl. A woman with graying

hair. BUT she wore a red rose on the rumpled brown lapel of her coat. So deep was my longing for the woman who's spirit had captured me that I approached her. There she stood, face was gentle and sensible and her gray eyes had a twinkle. I didn't hesitate. My hand gripped the small worn blue leather book which was to identify me to her.

I squared my shoulders and saluted and held out the book to the woman while choking back the bitterness of disappointment. "I'm Lt. John Blanchard and you must be Miss Maynell. I am so glad to meet you. May I take you to dinner?"

The woman's face broadened into a smile. "I don't know what this is about, son," she answered, "but the young lady in the green suit who just went by, asked me to wear this rose. And she said if you were to ask me out to dinner I should tell you that she is waiting for you in the large restaurant across the street. She said it was some kind of test!"

Apparently Lt. John Blanchard passed the test! Would you?

Today's Quote: *The magic of first love is our ignorance that it can ever end!* —Disraeli

Today's Verse: But the fruit of the Spirit is love, joy, peace, patience, kindness, goodness, faithfulness, gentleness and self-control (Gal. 5:22-23).

Day 3
Ten Commandments for a Successful Marriage

Everybody from "Dear Abby" on down through just about any publication you want to read will have some kind of a version of "Ten Commandments for Women" or "Ten Commandments for Men." Well . . . since we are on an equal footing, being partners in living, how about this version, the same set of commandments for both genders:

I. Put your mate before your mother, your father, your son and daughter, for your mate is your lifelong companion.

II. Do not abuse your body with excessive food, tobacco, drugs, or drink, so that your life may be long and healthy, in the presence of those you love.

III. Do not permit your business or your hobby or your recreation to make you a stranger to your children, for the most precious gift a parent can give his or her family is the gift of time.

IV. Do not forget that cleanliness is a virtue.

V. Do not make your mate into a beggar, but willingly share with him or her your worldly goods and possessions.

VI. Remember to say, "I love you." For even though your love may be a constant, your mate yearns to hear those words from you more than any others. Say it often.

VII. Remember always that the approval of your mate is worth more than the admiring glances of a hundred strangers, so remain faithful and loyal to your mate, and forsake all the others.

VIII. Keep your home in good repair, keep your marriage alive, for out of it come the joys of old age, together.

IX. Forgive with grace. For who among us does not need to be forgiven and often?

X. Honor the Lord your God all the days of your life, and your children and grandchildren will grow up and also bless you.[1]

Well . . . there you have them. Not only interesting reading, but a plan of action! Words do us no good until they have been translated into an understandable language.

Maybe we should add #11 as well: You shall not hit your mate over the head with these commandments, but the keeping of these will be a willing act of love.

Today's Quote: *Love never asks how much must I do, but how much can I do.* — Frederick A. Agar

Today's Verse: Submit yourselves unto such, and to every one that helpeth with us, and laboureth (1 Cor. 16:16).

Day 4
B.C. Fully Described

There are many versions of this little story which has appeared in Kiwanis and Rotary bulletins, magazines . . . the original source is lost someplace in antiquity. Enjoy:

My friend is a rather old-fashioned lady, quite elegant and delicate, especially in her choice of language. She and her husband were planning a week-long camping trip, so she wrote to a campground for reservations. She didn't quite know how to ask about toilet facilities. She didn't want to write "toilet" in her letter. After much deliberation, she thought of the old-fashioned term, "Bathroom Commode." But, when she wrote it down she thought she was being too forward, rewrote the entire letter and referred to the bathroom commode as the B.C. "Does your campground have its own B.C.?" she asked in her letter.

Well, the campground owner wasn't old-fashioned at all and when he got this letter, he couldn't figure out what she was talking about. The "B.C." business had him stumped. After giving it much thought the owner decided that she must be asking about the location for the local Baptist Church, so he wrote the following reply:

Dear Madam: I regret very much the delay in answering your letter but I now take the pleasure of informing you that the B.C. is located six miles north of the campground. It is capable of seating 250 people at one time. I will admit that it is quite a distance away if you are in the habit of going regularly. No doubt you will be pleased to know that a great number of people take their lunches along and make a day of it. The last time my wife and I went was six months ago and it was so crowded that we had to stand up the whole time. Right now, there is a supper planned to raise money for more seats. It will be held in the basement of the B.C. I would like to say that it pains me that I am not able to go more regularly, but it is not for lack of desire on my part. As we grow older, it seems to be more of an effort, especially in cold weather.

If you do decide to come to our campground, perhaps I could go with you the first time that you go, sit with you, and introduce you to all the other folks. Remember, that this is a very friendly community.

The Campground Owner

Oh, well . . . what more can be added than to tell you that it's okay for couples to share a good laugh together! And do it often!

Today's Quote: *A very good thing to have in your marriage is a funny bone!*

Today's Verse: A cheerful heart is good medicine, but a crushed spirit dries up the bones (Prov. 17:22).

Day 5
Revenge of Love

Newspaper columnist and minister George Crane tells of a wife who came into his office full of hatred toward her husband. "I do not only want to get rid of him, I want to get even. Before I divorce him, I want to hurt him as much as he has me!"

Dr. Crane suggested an ingenious plan: "Go home and act as if you really love your husband. Tell him how much he means to you. Praise him for every decent trait. Go out of your way to be as kind, considerate, and generous as possible. Spare no efforts to please him, to enjoy him. Make him believe you love him. After you've convinced him of your undying love and that you cannot live without him, drop the bomb. Tell him you are getting a divorce. That will really hurt him."

With revenge in her eyes, she smiled and exclaimed, "Beautiful! Beautiful! Will he ever be surprised!"

And she did it with enthusiasm. Acting "as if." For two months she showed love, kindness, listening, giving, reinforcing, sharing. . . .

When she didn't return, Dr. Crane called, "Are you ready now to go through with the divorce?"

"Divorce?" she exclaimed. "Never! I discovered I really do love him!"[2]

Is it really possible that actions can change feelings? From this story it appears so, but more than that, it's also a life concept. It's called the "as if" principle. This was first discovered and encouraged by Dr. Will James early in this century. It simply means that when you act "as if," you are enthused (for example), soon, feelings will follow your actions.

Let's try this definition for what love is and does: Love is an action directed to another person that is motivated by our relationship to Jesus Christ and is given freely without a personal reward in mind.[3]

Love, when applied to life situations, is the factor which makes our home operate smoothly. Love is always the oil in any kind of human relationship. Love is the key to making your home a much more pleasant place in which to live. You may not always "feel" like loving or being loving . . . but remember that your actions of love can change the feelings and emotions of love! Let your loving actions lead the way in your living!

Today's Quote: *People need love and need it most especially when they do not deserve it.*

Today's Verse: "Let us not love with words or tongue but with actions and in truth (1 John 3:18).

Day 6
Real Love

Moses Mendelssohn, the grandfather of the well-known German composer, was not handsome. He had a grotesque hunchback.

One day he visited a merchant in Hamburg who had a lovely daughter named Frumtje. Moses fell hopelessly in love with her. But Frumtje was repulsed by his misshapen appearance. When it came time for him to leave, Moses gathered his courage and climbed the stairs to her room to take one last opportunity to speak with her. She was a vision of heavenly beauty. After several attempts at conversation, Moses shyly asked, "Do you believe marriages are made in heaven?"

"Yes," she answered, looking at the floor. "And do you?"

"Yes, I do," he replied. "You see, in heaven at the birth of each boy, the Lord announces which girl he will marry. When I was born, my future bride was pointed out to me. Then the Lord added, 'But your wife will be humpbacked.'

"Right then and there I called out, 'Oh Lord, a humpbacked woman would be a tragedy. Please, Lord, give me the hump and let her be beautiful.' "

Then Frumtje looked up into his eyes and was stirred by some deep memory. She reached out and gave Mendelssohn her hand and later became his devoted wife.[4]

There's a wonderful line that describes this kind of love from the writings of the apostle Paul which says love "always protects, always trusts, always hopes, always perseveres."

Bennett Cerf relates this story about a bus that was bumping along a back road in the South. In one seat a wispy old man sat holding a bunch of fresh flowers. Across the aisle was a young girl whose eyes came back again and again to the man's flowers. The time came for the old man to get off. Impulsively he thrust the flowers into the girl's lap. "I can see you love the flowers," he explained, "and I think my wife would like for you to have them. I'll tell her I gave them to you." The girl accepted the flowers, then watched the old man get off the bus and walk through the gate of a small cemetery.

Love is a very special kind of gift . . . in order to be loved it is given without thought of a reward coming back. Let's always remember to love in action as well as in words.

Today's Quote: *The day will come when, after harnessing space, the winds, the tides, and gravitation, we shall harness for God the energies of love. And on that day, for the second time in the history of the world, we shall have discovered fire!* — Tielhard de Chardin

Today's Verse: And so we know and rely on the love God has for us. God is love. Whoever lives in love lives in God, and God in him (1 John 4:16).

Life's Most Embarrassing Moment

Grady Nutt, preacher and humorist, now deceased, told this story about a young family who invited the new pastor and his wife over for a get-acquainted Sunday dinner. The mother of the home was quite concerned that this be a perfect affair. She drilled the children days in advance about their proper behavior, what forks to use, when to use them, how to hold a napkin, and other important aspects of good manners.

Finally, the day arrived and the meal was prepared, and at exactly the right time everyone was invited to come into the dining room where the table was formally set with a white lace table cloth, the best china, good silverware, centerpiece, candles, and everything. They all sat down at the beautiful, formal table and the father said the blessing and when the blessing was over, their little nine-year-old daughter reached for her glass of iced tea and knocked it over!

The little brother jumped to get out of the way of the spilling tea and knocked his glass over, too! There was an awkward moment of silence as everybody sort of looked to the mother, realizing how disappointed she must be. She had gone to so much trouble and now there was this huge spreading stain in the middle of the white lace tablecloth.

But before anybody could say anything, the father flipped his glass of tea over, and began to laugh. The preacher caught on and flipped over his tea and started to laugh. The pastor's wife knocked over her glass of tea and joined the laughter. Then . . . everybody looked to the mother and finally with an expression of resignation she picked up her glass and just dumped it out in the middle of the table and everybody around the table roared with laughter.

And the father looked down at his nine-year-old daughter, right beside him, and he winked at her. And as she laughed embarrassedly, she looked up at her father and winked back, but as she did, it flicked a tear onto her cheek and it rolled down her face. She continued to look up, almost worshipfully, at a father who loved her enough to be sensitive to save her from one of life's most embarrassing moments.

One more time . . . love comes to the rescue! Love does not embarrass another. Such behavior should not be a part of our living together . . . whether directed to a spouse or children or extended family or any other friends! Love does not embarrass someone else! To embarrass another is to send a very mixed signal. How can you show love and at the same cause embarrassment?

Today's Quote: *Love that is really love will do all that is possible to avoid what may prove to be embarrassing to others.*

Today's Verse: Dear friends, since God so loved us, we also ought to love one another (1 John 4:11).

Day 8
The Kiss

Dr. Richard Selzer who is a surgeon, has written some very interesting human interest stories in one or more of his books, based on his life experiences as a doctor. One of my favorites is the following:

I stand by the bed where a young woman lies, her face post-operative, her mouth twisted in palsy, clownish. A tiny twig of the facial nerve, the one to the muscles of her mouth has been severed. She will be thus from now on. The surgeon had followed with religious fervor the curve of her flesh; I promise you that. Nevertheless, to remove the tumor from her cheek, I had cut the little nerve. Her young husband is in the room. He stands on the opposite side of the bed, and together they seem to dwell in the evening lamplight, isolated from me, private. *Who are they,* I ask myself, *he and this wry-mouth I have made, who gaze at and touch each other so generously, greedily?*

"Will my mouth always be like this?" she asks.

"Yes," I say, "it will be. It is because the nerve was cut."

She nods and is silent. But the young man smiles. "I like it," he says. "It is kind of cute."

All at once I know who he is. I understand, and I lower my gaze. One is not bold in an encounter with a god. Unmindful, he bends to kiss her crooked mouth, and I am so close I can see how he twists his own lips to accommodate hers, to show her that their kiss still works.[5]

Love that is love is considerate. It's putting others at ease. It's a time to lift the spirits of another. It's to help put aside any fears of the future. What a way to open the inside doors of the spirit of another.

In our story we see a special kind of loving, doing all that is possible to avoid what may prove to be a point of concern. It's also given at what may be a great sacrifice, going the second mile, doing the very nice thing, accommodating actions so that somebody precious may be spared more pain. One of the things being discovered about relationships and marriages is that when a handicapped child is born into a home, in about 80 percent of the cases, that home will eventually come to divorce because of the extra pain, problems, and hurts to overcome. Let's make the accommodations necessary . . . even with a kiss, if necessary!

Today's Quote: *Those who deserve love least, need it most!* — Eleanor Doan

Today's Verse: So I will very gladly spend for you everything I have and expend myself as well. If I love you more, will you love me less? (2 Cor. 12:15).

Day 9
The Dramatic Change

Larry and Jo Ann were an ordinary couple. They lived in an ordinary house on an ordinary street. They struggled to make ends meet and to do the right things for their children. They were ordinary in yet another way . . . they had their squabbles. Much of their conversation concerned what was wrong in their marriage and who was to blame. Until one day when a most extraordinary event took place.

"You know, Jo Ann, I've got a magic chest of drawers. Every time I open them, they're full of socks and underwear," Larry said. "I want to thank you for filling them all these years."

Jo Ann stared at her husband over the top of her glasses. "What do you want, Larry?"

"I just want you to know I appreciate those magic drawers."

Jo Ann pushed the incident out of her mind until a few days later.

"Jo Ann, thank you for recording so many correct check numbers in the ledger this month. You put down the right numbers 15 out of 16 times. That's a record."

Disbelieving what she had heard, Jo Ann looked up from her mending. "Larry, you're always complaining about my recording the wrong check numbers. Why stop now?"

"No reason. I just wanted you to know I appreciate the effort."

Jo Ann shook her head and went back to her mending. *What's got into him?* she thought.

She tried to disregard it, but Larry's strange behavior intensified.

"Jo Ann, that was a great dinner," he said one evening. "I appreciate all your effort. Why, in the past 15 years I'll bet you've fixed over 14,000 meals for me and the kids."

Then, "Jo Ann, the house looks spiffy." And even, "Thanks, Jo Ann, for just being you. I really enjoy your company."

Jo Ann was growing worried. *Where's the sarcasm, the criticism?*

But Jo Ann's step was now a little lighter.

That would be the end of the story except one day another extraordinary event took place. This time it was Jo Ann who spoke.

"Larry," she said, "I want to thank you for going to work and providing for us all these years. I don't think I've ever told you how much I appreciate it."

Larry never revealed the reason for his dramatic change of behavior . . . but it's one I'm thankful to live with.

You see, I am Jo Ann.[6]

Today's Quote: *The chance for appreciation is much increased by being the child of an appreciator.* — Ralph Waldo Emerson

Today's Verse: A word aptly spoken is like apples of gold in settings of silver (Prov. 25:11).

Day 10
A Courageous Woman

In 1921 Lewis Lawes became the warden at Sing Sing Prison. No prison was tougher than Sing Sing during that time. But when Warden Lawes retired some 20 years later, that prison had become a humanitarian institution. Those who studied the system said credit for the change belong to Lawes. But when he was asked about the transformation, here's what he said: "I owe it all to my wonderful wife, Catherine, who is buried outside the prison walls."

Catherine Lawes was a young mother with three small children when her husband became the warden. Everybody warned her from the beginning that she should never set foot inside the prison walls, but that didn't stop Catherine! When the first prison basketball game was held, she went . . . walking into the gym with her three beautiful kids and she sat in the stands with the inmates. Her attitude was: "My husband and I are going to take care of these men and I believe they will take care of me! I don't have to worry!"

She insisted on getting acquainted with them and their records. She discovered one convicted murderer was blind so she paid him a visit. Holding his hand in hers she said, "Do you read Braille?"

"What's Braille?" he asked. Then she taught him how to read. Years later he would weep in love for her.

Later, Catherine found a deaf-mute in prison. She went to school to learn how to use sign language. Many said that Catherine Lawes was the body of Jesus that came alive again in Sing Sing from 1921 to 1937.

Then, she was killed in a car accident. The next morning Lewis Lawes didn't come to work, so the acting warden took his place. It seemed almost instantly that the prison knew something was wrong.

The following day her body was resting in a casket in her home, three-quarters of a mile from the prison. As the acting warden took his early morning walk he was shocked to see a large crowd of the toughest, hardest-looking criminals gathered like a herd of animals at the main gate. He came closer and noted tears of grief and sadness. He knew how much they loved Catherine. He turned and faced the men, "All right, men, you can go. Just be sure and check in tonight!" Then he opened the gate and a parade of criminals walked, without a guard, the three-quarters of a mile to stand in line to pay their final respects to Catherine Lawes. And every one of them checked back in. Every one!

The power of love never ceases to amaze me, especially when we see it in a person like Catherine. It's amazing what one life can accomplish when that person believes in others!

Today's Quote: *There are no hopeless cases, only hopeless thinkers!*

Today's Verse: But God demonstrates His own love for us in this: While we were still sinners, Christ died for us (Rom. 5:8).

Day 11
Record-Breaking Love

Robert Ripley, of "Believe-It-or-Not" fame writes about the "world's longest love letter." Mr. Ripley declares that the longest, and maybe the simplest, love letter ever written was the work of a very romantic French artist named Marcel de Leclure. In 1875 he undertook the task of sending Magdelene de Villalore this communiqué which expressed his deep feelings for her. It was quite simple in content. How effective it was is anybody's guess.

What Leclure's letter contained was the phrase "Jevous Aime" — in English, "I love you." This phrase was written 1,875,000 times! That's all! 1,875,000 "I love you's"! His plan was to write this message 1,000 times for each year of the calendar to date. So we have the year 1875 times 1,000 to arrive at his romantic love letter!

Leclure did not write this letter in his own hand. No . . . he hired a secretary, a scribe, in that day. But this prodigious lover must have been entranced by the words. Therefore he dictated the letter to the scribe word for word, verbatim for the entire letter!

Then he had the scribe repeat the letter back to him word for word each time he wrote the phrase! By our calculations, this phrase was uttered by mouth and in written form 5,625,000 times before it was sent! What a monumental task! And I wonder how much this letter weighed when finished, or how many pages it filled up!? What did the lady, Magdelene de Villalore, say when this was delivered to her? How long did it take? Did they ever marry?

There are spouses who never utter these words. Mr. Ripley adds this tidbit as his commentary: "Never was love made manifest by as great an expenditure of time and effort." This Frenchman must have been something else, and his effort must be appreciated. But I happen to think that Mr. Ripley was wrong in his statement.

Something else comes to mind. Did he do anything else except write out and speak out his love for Magdelene? Love, to be love, must be much more than mere words, no matter how many million times you may say or write it. Actions better express love than words. I'm not downplaying the words, but the two must go together, words and actions. Actions and words. Love is to be expressed as well as acted out. Really, you can never tell someone "I love you" too often. Let's make it a habit of our relationship. One of the saddest emotions felt is love that is never expressed. So, what are you waiting for? Tell that one you love, "I LOVE YOU!" NOW!

Today's Quote: *I love you!* — Marcel de Leclure

Today's Verse: Forsake her not, and she shall preserve thee: love her, and she shall keep thee (Prov. 4:6).

Day 12
Ten Million Dollar Caper

Imagine, if you can, that you have sent in your entry for the "Publisher's Clearing House" contest for the ten million dollar grand prize . . . and you are notified you have won! While we're on this subject, if I were a gambling person I'd be willing to bet that most of us are diligent about sending back the entries for those delectable grand prizes. Well, we can at least dream. Back to our story.

Larry Whitaker, who is the advertising director at the Springfield, Missouri, *News Leader* (daily newspaper), was interrupted one morning at the office with the presentation of a huge TEN MILLION DOLLAR check from Publisher's Clearing House. There were official check presenters, they had arrived in the official van with the "prize patrol" insignia on the side, reporters were present along with TV cameras! What a happy occasion! TEN MILLION DOLLARS! And Larry Whitaker was already mentally spending the check. The activities had proceeded from inside the office to outside on the front sidewalk of the *News Leader* building. A small crowd was looking on and enjoying the good fortune of one of their own!

Then his wife, Charlene, mysteriously appeared, holding a huge bouquet of flowers, and walked over to Larry with a huge smile on her face, grabbed him around the neck, and whispered in his ear, "April Fool!"

All of this was just one huge April Fools' Day prank which had been perpetrated by the *News Leader* publisher, Fritz Jacobi, and many friends who pitched in, along with wife Charlene. Fritz Jacobi said, "We just felt the ultimate prankster deserved the ultimate payback, and he got it!" And the two later played three hours of golf together.

"So we're still talking," Whitaker said, "but it's going to be fun getting even!"[7]

Into the life of every couple . . . some fun must fall! Life without a laughter break once in a while can get pretty grim. It's okay to laugh! In fact, it should be made a requirement for each couple to learn to laugh together.

To "laugh" is to chuckle, giggle, roar, chortle, guffaw, snicker, titter, cackle, break up, roll in the aisle, howl, make merry, be joyful, belly laugh, and to split one's side! And in today's world there is a laughter dearth! Over time, chuckling this much also lowers blood pressure and heart rate, reduces pain, strengthens the immune system, and cuts down on stress-creating hormones. Biggest problem: finding that many things to laugh about!"

Today's Quote: *Laughter is a joy flowing, happiness showing, countenance glowing, kind of attitude.*"

Today's Verse: The One enthroned in heaven laughs" (Ps. 2:4).

Day 13
Why the Doctor Was Too Late

It was almost one in the morning when the phone rang in the Winter's home. Dr. Leo Winters, the highly acclaimed Chicago surgeon, was awakened with a start.

Tonight it was a young boy, they said, tragically mangled in a late-night accident. Could not someone else handle it? Not this time. This time his hands were possibly the only ones in the city, or maybe even in the whole region, which were skilled enough to save a life.

The quickest route happened to be through a rather tough area, but with time being a critical factor, it was worth the risk. Then, at a stop light, his door was jerked open by a man in a gray hat and a dirty flannel shirt. "I've got to have your car!" the man screamed, pulling the doctor from his seat. Winters tried explaining the gravity of his situation, but the man was not listening.

The doctor wandered for over 45 minutes looking for a phone. When the taxi finally got him to the hospital, over an hour had passed. He burst through the doors and into the nurses' station but the nurse on duty only shook her head. Too late. The boy had died about 30 minutes earlier. "His dad got here just before he died," the nurse told him. "He is in the chapel. Go see him. He is awfully confused. He could not understand why you never came."

Without explaining, Dr. Winters walked hurriedly down the hall and entered the chapel. At the front knelt the huddled form of a weeping father, in a gray hat and dirty flannel shirt. Tragically, he had pushed from his life the only one who could have saved the life of his son![8]

As I have written down this story, I also have the strangest feeling that somewhere in the past I have known that same father. With a marriage coming apart at the seams, he just could not find time for his wife or to spend cultivating a relationship with the Lord of life. With a business rapidly sliding downhill, he will further put off a decision about Jesus Christ. Tragically, and too late, there is a tendency to push away some of the only sources of help we have access to in our desperate time of need. It's best to be prepared for the worst — with relationships in order, on a steady walk with God, working on marital harmony on an on-going basis, keeping things clear between ourselves and our kids. Hindsight is always 20/20, but the problem with that is life is not lived in reverse . . . it's in forward, and to most of us it's fast-forward. Therefore, let's keep short accounts!

Today's Quote: *All the troubles of life come upon us because we refuse to sit quietly for a while each day in our rooms.* — Blaise Pascal

Today's Verse: The righteous man is rescued from trouble, and it comes on the wicked instead (Prov. 11:8).

Statistical Nonsense

There really is good news for the American family! You have heard all about the glum statistics that say one out of two marriages will end in divorce. You've read that half of all marriages end in divorce! Not! Wrong! According to pollster Louis Harris, only one in eight marriages will end in divorce!

Americans have been led to believe for the last decade that the institution of marriage is decaying, since the government's National Center for Health Statistics revealed that there had been 2.4 million new marriages and 1.2 million divorces in 1981. Overlooked in calculating the divorce statistics was the number of already existing marriages.

"What was left out is that there are 54 million other marriages that are going on very nicely, thank you," Harris said. Each year ONLY 2 PERCENT of existing marriages will actually end in divorce, according to calculations by Harris which combine ongoing and new marriages. A statistician with the U.S. Census Bureau agreed that the divorce statistics presented for the last few years have been deceiving because the number of ongoing marriages were not calculated.

"A number of academics made a sensational splash out of the statistics released in 1981," Harris said, "and the media got a lot of mileage out of it. Ever since then, an indelible message has been chorused in church pulpits, academic broadsides, and political prophecies of doom for the American family. In reality, the American family is surviving under enormous pressure."

Harris questioned the much-touted divorce statistics after polling 3,001 persons for a family survey. The study showed a "glowing picture of the American family."

Among the findings of the poll:

85 percent of American families have happy marriages!

94 percent are highly satisfied with family relationships!

86 percent said they are happy with the support they receive from family members during a crisis!

Twenty percent, ONLY 20 PERCENT, said they are not happy with their family life!

Harris called the one-out-of-two divorce-marriage ratio "one of the most specious pieces of statistical nonsense ever perpetrated in modern times!"[9] THEREFORE . . . never again tell anyone that one of two marriages ends in divorce! And decide that yours will not be one of the few that eventually does!

Today's Quote: *All weddings are happy . . . it's the living together afterwards that is tough.*

Today's Verse: Submit to one another out of reverence for Christ (Eph. 5:21).

Day 15
The Spice of Wife

With the world spinning so fast and friendships being so few, a marriage may be the only stable and secure commitment a couple will know throughout their hurried life. It must be put on a higher priority if a person wants to enjoy rest over the long haul. John Fischer, a Christian musician, offers some sound advice along these lines. It seems that John had rented a room from an elderly couple who had been married longer than most people get a chance to live.

But even though time had wrinkled their hands, stooped their postures, and slowed them down, it hadn't diminished the excitement and love they felt toward each other. John could tell that their love had not stopped growing since the day of their wedding . . . over a half century before.

Intrigued, the singer finally had an opportunity to ask the old man the secret to his success as a husband.

"Oh," said the old gentleman with a twinkle in his eye, "that's simple. Just bring her roses on Wednesday . . . she never expects them then."

The conversation inspired a song:

> Give her roses on Wednesday, when everything is blue,
> Roses are red and your love must be new.

Give her roses on Wednesday, keep it shining through,
Love her when love's the hardest thing to do.
Love isn't something you wait for,
Like some feeling creeping up from behind.
Love's a decision to give more,
And keep giving all of the time.
Give her roses on Wednesday.

It's easy to love when it's easy,
When you're in a Friday frame of mind.
But loving when living gets busy,
Is what love was waiting for all the time.
Give her roses on Wednesday.[10]

Today's Quote: *How much the wife is dearer than the bride.* — George, Lord Lyttelton

Today's Verse: Husbands, love your wives and do not be harsh with them (Col. 3:19).

Day 16
Love Listens

This is how a military officer loved his wife out of a mental hospital. The psychiatrist had prescribed that his wife be admitted to the local mental hospital. He was stunned and challenged, but had no idea how to help her. He sought counsel from the chaplain and learned he should allow his wife to sit in his lap and share her true feelings about him.

He followed this advice with great difficulty because it hurt to hear the things she said he was doing to weaken their marriage. As she was talking, the telephone rang and he felt "saved by the bell." She was angry because she thought he would probably not return. But she overheard one statement he made that not only kept her from a breakdown, but prompted her to slip into a nightgown and actually desire to arouse him (something she had not done in years). After the call, she calmly snuggled back into his lap.

What had he said to his commanding officer?

He simply said, "Sir, could someone else take that assignment tonight? I'm in the middle of a very important time with my wife. It's serious and I really don't want to leave at this point."

That military officer had begun to prove to his wife that she was of high value to him. As a result, her mental condition stabilized . . . and she never had to go to the hospital![11]

Intimacy and attention . . . are they really that powerful in a relationship? Here's another interesting tidbit about a woman's capacity for intimacy . . . and therefore, her potential for a successful male relationship. This is directly linked to her father. A study of 7,000 women who worked in strip joints or topless bars revealed that most of the women came from "absent-father" homes. The researcher, Christopher P. Anderson, commented, "Most of these women conceded that they were probably looking for the male attention that they had never gotten during their childhood. Lacking that foundation, many of these women also admitted that they did not rely on men for intimacy."[12]

"Intimacy" is closeness, familiarity, caring, tenderness, fondness, dearness, affection, warmth, endearment, camaraderie, and lovemaking. It's something to be worked at because it just doesn't simply happen. It seems to come easier for women to do but is something that must be a real goal in relationships which men need to work on. It's powerful, it's therapeutic, it's bonding, it's a part of real love in action.

Today's Quote: *A successful marriage requires falling in love many times, always with the same person.* — Mignon McLaughlin

Today's Verse: I am my lover's and my lover is mine (Song of Sol. 6:3).

Day 17
'Til Death Do Us Part

In John Hersey's novel, *The Wall,* there occurs a haunting scene. This is a novel about the Polish Jews and the Nazis, and while it is a novel in form, the episodes are based upon actual events. In this particular episode, John Hersey tells how the diabolical Nazis shipped Jews from the Warsaw ghetto to different concentration camps. A long column of men and women is passing in front of a Nazi officer.

If a person looks fit, the officer sends him to another line, for work in a factory. If not, he goes to the death line. A man and wife, middle-aged, are in the column. They are quarreling venomously. Some irritation had become big as all life. Perhaps they are blaming each other for their plight. If their quarreling seems out of place, it is also understandable. In the face of danger confronting them, and their probable fate, all reserve and reticence have fled. Reason has left.

Finally, the two arrive in front of the Nazi. He looks them over briefly and motions the man to the working line. The wife he sends to death. For a moment the man stands alone. Then, with a sob, he leaves his haven and slowly walks over to his wife. They stand together, wordlessly, and then they go off to death . . . together.[13]

Most wedding ceremonies have at their core this promise, "For better, for worse, for richer, for poorer, in sickness and in health, to love, and to cherish . . . till death do us part." Then, we, the participants, the promisers, the covenanters, are called upon to make it permanent! It sounds simple enough at the time of the promise, but the living it out in good and bad times, through thick and thin, can only be done in total commitment!

Have you ever given thought to the first miracle of Jesus in His ministry? It was a wedding! It was a miracle of turning the water into wine to prolong the wedding party. It was a miracle of joy! To me, this is a strong indication that Jesus Christ is also interested in your marriage and the life which follows. It was done to bring joy to a host, hostess, the bride and groom, and their guests! God cares enough to have sent His Son to help people have fun and He cares enough about you and your home to also be a welcomed guest! It's not until we get tired of each other . . . it's until death parts us! That's the covenant, and the choice is yours. The grace to pull it off comes from Him, the most honored wedding guest.

Today's Quote: *Hasty marriage seldom proveth well.* — William Shakespeare, from King Henry VI

Today's Verse: My command is this: Love each other as I have loved you. Greater love has no one than this, that he lay down his life for his friends (John 15:12-13).

Day 18
Love That Transcends

Sir Thomas More was an Irish poet. He married, early in life, a beautiful Irish lass. Her beauty was such that no one looking at her could fail to take note of her flaming red hair and green eyes. She and Sir Thomas were very happy, experiencing the heights and probing the depths of their intimacy on every level.

The time came when Sir Thomas was called away from home for a time. During his absence his lovely wife contracted the dread disease smallpox. And you know what scars this disease leaves. What had once been the loveliest of faces now became an ugly desecration of that loveliness. And she was so fearful of Sir Thomas's rejection that she resolved in her heart that he would never again see her face by the light of day. She kept herself in her room and had heavy drapes fitted for the bedroom to block out all the rays of the sun.

Sir Thomas returned late one evening. He was informed by the household staff of what had happened to his once lovely wife. He went to their bedroom, came to the door, opened it, entered, and began to move in the direction of the bed. She recognized his footsteps and said, "No, Thomas, come no nearer. I have resolved that you will never see me again by the light of day." Sir Thomas stopped, hesitated, and without saying a word turned and left the room.

He descended and moved to the music room where he sat at the piano working on the words of a poem. Through the night he labored, until early in the morning he folded the piece of paper, placed it in his vest, and returned to the stairs. He came to the door of the bedroom, pushed it open, and there in the hallway he read the poem:

> Believe me, if all those endearing young charms,
> Which I look on so fondly today, were to pass in a moment,
> And flee from my arms like fairy dreams fading away,
> Thou would'st still be adored, as this moment thou art.
> Let thy loveliness fade as it will;
> And around that dear visage each throb of my heart
> Would entwine itself verdantly still.

He finished reading the poem and threw open the heavy drapes. As he did the first rays of the early morning's light flooded into the room. He turned just in time to receive her into his arms and there the two of them knew the embrace that only those who truly love can know.[14]

Today's Quote: *It is strange that men will talk of miracles, revelations, inspiration, and the like, as things past, while love remains.* — Henry David Thoreau

Today's Verse: Many waters cannot quench love; rivers cannot wash it away. If one were to give all the wealth of his house for love, it would be utterly scorned (Song of Sol. 8:7).

Day 19
Love from the Heart

Love affairs are not unusual for young teenagers today. It's not particularly surprising when such love affairs are broken for some reason or another. Normally, teens get over the hurt they feel for a broken relationship and discover that there are other "fish in the sea."

This very typical pattern of teen love began as Felipe Garza Jr. began dating Donna Ashlock. Felipe was 15 and Donna was 14. They dated until Donna cooled the romance and began dating other boys.

One day, Donna doubled over in pain. Doctors soon discovered that Donna was dying of degenerative heart disease and desperately needed a heart transplant. Felipe heard about Donna's condition and told his mother, "I'm going to die and I'm going to give my heart to my girlfriend." Boys say some irrational things like this from time to time. After all, Felipe appeared to his mom to be in perfect health.

Three weeks later, Felipe woke up and complained of pain on the left side of his head. He began losing his breath and couldn't walk. He was taken to a hospital where it was discovered that a blood vessel in his brain had burst and left him brain dead. Felipe's sudden death mystified his doctors! While he remained on a respirator, his family decided to let physicians remove his heart for Donna and his kidneys and eyes for others in need of those organs.

Donna received Felipe's heart! After the transplant, Donna's father told her that Felipe had evidently been sick for about three months before he had died. He said, "He donated his kidneys and eyes." There was a pause and Donna said, "And I have his heart."

Her father said, "Yes, that was what he and his parents wished." Her expression changed just a little. She then asked her father who knew. He told her, "Everybody." Nothing else was said.

Several days later, a funeral procession seemed to roll on forever through the orchards and fields of Patterson, California. The procession was so long it might have been that of a prince, but it was Felipe. His only claim to fame was his love and his heart. It's unforgettable when a person gives up his life so that someone he loves can live. It would be unforgettable if you had received a new and healthy heart from someone who loved you more than you could appreciate. Every moment you lived would be a tribute and testimony to the one who loved you so much that they gave their life for you.[15]

Think a moment . . . and make whatever life application comes to mind.

Today's Quote: *Love is the key to the universe which unlocks all doors.*

Today's Verse: Blessed are the pure in heart: for they shall see God (Matt. 5:8).

Day 20
Eternal Gain

Russ Chandler, religion writer for the *Los Angeles Times,* wrote an excellent book a few years ago in which he tells the stories of 12 outstanding Christians who have dealt with significant problems in their lives. The book begins with Elisabeth Elliot, who first became prominent through her account of the martyrdom of the five young missionaries who were murdered by the Auca Indians in 1956, including her husband Jim Elliot. She recalled some of the trying events of her life through which she learned important lessons.

Elisabeth, who first went to South America to do translation work in 1952, mentioned three experiences of loss in that first year working with a small tribe of Indians called the Colorados. The first calamity was the murder of the informant who was giving her information about the language and culture of the Colorados.

A second catastrophe was the loss of all the work Elisabeth did that year. All her files, tapes, notebooks, and vocabulary compilations were stolen and no copies or duplicates existed. The same year, Jim was reconstructing a small jungle mission station among the Quichua Indians. During a sudden flood one night, all of the buildings he had rebuilt, plus three new ones, were swept away down the Amazon River.

These three experiences of total earthly loss taught Elisabeth and

Jim the deep lessons that Jesus taught His disciples: "Truly, I say unto you, unless a grain of wheat falls into the earth and dies, it remains alone; but if it dies, it bears much fruit" (John 12:24;RSV). The practical outcome of that lesson was this, according to Elisabeth: "I had to face up to the fact in those stunning losses that God was indeed sovereign; therefore, He was my Lord, my Master, the One in charge of my life, the One who deserved my worship and my service. The road to eternal gain leads inevitably through earthly loss. True faith is operative in the dark. True faith deals with the inexplicable things of life. If we have explanations . . . if things are clear and simple . . . there's not very much need for faith.

"Through these three experiences of loss we came to know Jesus Christ in a deeper way and began to enter into the lessons that Paul describes."[16]

Life is not fair. But there also is no gain without pain or loss.

Today's Quote: *The things which seem to break us are the things which really make us.*

Today's Verse: But whatever was to my profit I now consider loss for the sake of Christ. What is more, I consider everything a loss compared to the surpassing greatness of knowing Christ Jesus my Lord, for whose sake I have lost all things" (Phil. 3:7-8).

Day 21
The Last "I Love You"

Carol's husband was killed in an accident last year. Jim, only 52, was driving home from work. The other driver was a teenager with a very high blood-alcohol level. Jim died instantly. The teenager was in the emergency room less than two hours.

There were other ironic twists: It was Carol's fiftieth birthday, and Jim had two plane tickets to Hawaii in his pocket. He was going to surprise her. Instead, he was killed by a drunken driver. "How have you survived this?" I finally asked Carol, a year later.

Her eyes welled up with tears. I thought I had said the wrong thing, but she gently took my hand and said, "It's all right, I want to tell you. The day I married Jim, I promised I would never let him leave the house in the morning without telling him I loved him. He made the same promise. It got to be a joke between us, and as babies came along it got to be a hard promise to keep. I remember running down the driveway, saying 'I love you' through clenched teeth when I was mad, or driving to the office to put a note in his car. It was a funny challenge.

"We made a lot of memories trying to say 'I love you' before noon every day of our married life. The morning Jim died, he left a birthday card in the kitchen and slipped out to the car. I heard the engine starting. *Oh, no, you don't buster,* I thought. I raced out and banged on the car window until he rolled it down. 'Here on my fiftieth birthday, Mr. James E. Garret, I, Carol Garret, want to go on record as saying I love you!' That's how I've survived. Knowing that the last words I said to Jim were 'I LOVE YOU!' "[17]

If you love somebody . . . tell them, NOW! Give them a call . . . drive to the office . . . send a special card . . . write a love note . . . rent a billboard . . . charter a sky-writing plane . . . buy a dozen roses . . . bring a box of candy . . . buy a book . . . do a back rub . . . plant a tree . . . make a favorite meal . . . buy the special dress . . . do the dishes . . . whisper it in the ear . . . pack a note in the lunch box . . . secure a coveted CD. Be imaginative, be creative, but do it NOW! If you love someone, tell them in ways that they will understand to be an expression of love!

Together, how about making this our daily prayer: "Lord, please remind me today and every day to say 'I LOVE YOU' out loud to the people whom I live with and whom I love! And, Lord, please help me to remember to put this love into actions which they will interpret as being acts of love!"

Today's Quote: *Love is an action directed to another person that is motivated by our relationship to Jesus Christ and is given freely without a personal reward in mind.*

Today's Verse: Love never fails (1 Cor. 13:8).

Day 22
Something Different

A housewife called the Sanitation Department in her town to come out and please pick up a dead mule from the front of her house. The department sent out several men and a truck to do the cleanup. Then she changed her mind. She came running out to the crew and asked the men to take the dead mule upstairs and place it in the bathtub. "I'll give you $20 each for doing this little job," she said.

The crew didn't really understand. However, $20 is $20, so they began the task. After much struggle and heavy lifting they finally managed to get the mule upstairs and deposited in the bathtub. It was quite a feat. When the task had been finished and she was giving each of the crew their hard-earned $20, the foreman asked, "Ma'am, why did you want this dead mule placed in your bathtub? Thank you for the $20, but why?"

"Well," she replied, "my husband has come home every night for the past 35 years and has gone through the same routine without change. He will pull off his coat and shoes. He grabs the newspaper, sits down in his easy chair, and always asks, "What's new?" In those 35 years there has never been anything new, so tonight I'm going to tell him!" Can you just imagine what kind of a reaction that poor old guy will have to this news?

Life really is exciting! For too many of us life has been the same old routine, same old sixes and sevens, the same ho-hum, nothing different, nothing new, and that's so sad.

There's an epitaph chiseled in a gravestone some place in the New England states with this inscription: "This man died at twenty-one, but was buried at seventy-three!"

Something new or exciting in your life is not dependent upon your chronological age, either. It was my privilege to visit with a senior citizen a few years ago. At that time he was 78 years of age, and I asked him what he was planning to do. "Well," he said, with a twinkle in his eye, "this next year I'm going to learn how to become a sculptor!"

You've heard the old adage "You can't teach an old dog new tricks." Have you given it a try? You can teach an old dog new tricks with a simple technique called "behavior modification." Consider a job change or forming a new and better habit. There's excitement ahead! Plan something different. TODAY!

Today's Quote: *None are so old as those who have outlived their enthusiasm!* — Henry David Thoreau

Today's Verse: The thief comes only in order to steal, kill, and destroy. I have come in order that they [you] might have life, life in all its fullness (John 10:10;TEV).

Day 23
Years in Waiting

Did you know that most people spend an average of about five years of their lives just standing in lines? What kinds of lines? Grocery checkout, driver's license renewal, cafeteria, restaurant, ticket window, subway station, and so forth. That's not all. Most people spend a total of six months of their life waiting at stop lights!

"Most people don't realize how much time they're wasting," said Michael Fortino, president of the consulting firm, Priority Management Pittsburgh, Inc. To determine how people spend their time and where they spend their time, Priority Management researchers, often with a stopwatch and clipboard in hand, studied hundreds of people across this nation for more than a year.

The study was released in 1988, after a year's research. This time-use study estimated the average person spends six months at stop lights, eight months opening junk mail, one year searching for misplaced objects, two years attempting to return phone calls to people who never seem to be available, four years doing housework, five years in lines, and six years eating.

"The whole point is to spend time doing the things that you want to do rather than the things you dislike," said Mr. Fortino.

The study of time usage is an interesting subject because everyone of us has the same exact allotment of time. Yes, I know, perhaps not in the length of our living, but in the sense that each of us has an exact total of 24 hours in each day and 156 hours in each week. Time is also a non-renewable commodity. There is not one minute of your life that can be lived more than once.

When we were growing up as little ones, time seemed to drag . . . minutes seemed endless . . . but now the minutes flash past, but the years seem long. Have you ever given any serious thought as to how you invest your time? Perhaps a study like Priority Management's will help us think about it.

While we're on the subject, have you thought about "tithing" your time as well as your money? There are 156 hours in a week and a tithe would be 15.6 hours. If you attend church twice on Sunday that may account for about 5 hours, and throw in another 3 for a mid-week activity for church, and you still have 7.6 hours left! Where would be a good place to make this investment of your time? How about helping a neighbor or sick friend?

Today's Quote: *Fifteen minutes a day devoted to one definite study will make one a master in a dozen years.* — Edward H. Griggs

Today's Verse: Be very careful, then, how you live . . . not as unwise but as wise, making the most of every opportunity (Eph. 5:15-16).

Day 24
The Battle of Selfishness

A farmer's son decided to get married. When his dad heard the news he said, "John, when you get married your liberty is gone!" The son questioned this and refused to believe it. The dad said, "I'll prove it to you. Catch a dozen chickens, tie them up, put them in the wagon, and go to town. Stop at every house and wherever you find the husband is boss give him a horse. Wherever you find the woman is boss, give her a chicken. You'll give away all your chickens and you'll come back with your team of horses intact."

John accepted the proposition and drove to town. He stopped at every house and had given away 10 chickens when he came to a very nice little house. The old man and his wife were standing out in front on the lawn. He called to them and asked, "Who is the boss in your house?"

The man replied, "I am."

He turned to the lady and she said, "Yes, he's really the boss."

John was excited with the prospect of establishing the boss in this home, so he invited them to come down into the street; explained his proposition and told them to select one of the horses. The old man and his wife looked them over carefully and the husband finally said, "I think the black is the better. I choose him."

The wife said, "I think the bay horse is the better. I'd choose him."

The old man took another careful look at the bay horse and said, "I guess I'll take the bay horse."

John smiled and said, "No you won't, you'll take a chicken!"

Selfishness is a constant battle and no one can successfully master this conflict without outside help! Some of the most unselfish people I have known are in a lifelong struggle against selfishness.

A circus had a lion and a lamb in the same cage. A man asked the attendant if they got along all right. The attendant replied, "Most of the time, if we keep the lion well fed. . . . Now and then we have to put in a new lamb."

In the conflicts of life you are facing there is only one road to victory! That's found in Jesus Christ! Victory is won when we strive to be, say, and do what God wants us to be, say, and do. Then we, too, will live in victory over conflict — not in our strength, but in His strength! The bottom line will be determined in how well you handle this conflict in resolution.

Today's Quote: *Life lived at its best will include an arena of conflict as well as victory over conflict!* — Robert J. Strand

Today's Verse: I can do everything through Him who gives me strength (Phil. 4:13).

Day 25
Footprints

Wayne Watson has put music to the words and perhaps you've heard him or another gospel artist sing it lately. The author of these beautiful words is unknown, so we cannot give credit where it is due. Nevertheless, it conveys a timeless message that you may need to hear on a day like this. It's entitled, "Footprints In the Sand."

One night I had a dream. I dreamed I was walking along the beach with the Lord and across the sky flashed scenes from my life. For each scene I noticed two sets of footprints in the sand. One belonged to me and the other to the Lord.

When the last scene of my life flashed before us I looked back at the footprints in the sand. I noticed that many times along the path of my life there was only one set of footprints. I also noticed that it happened at the very lowest and saddest times in my life.

This really bothered me and I questioned the Lord about it. "Lord, you said that once I decided to follow You, You would walk with me all the way. But I noticed that during the most troublesome times in my life there was only one set of footprints. I don't understand why, in times when I needed You most, You should leave me."

The Lord replied, "My precious, precious child. I love you and I would never, never leave you during your times of trial and suffering. When you saw only one set of footprints . . . it was then that I carried you!"

What an exciting expression of God's love and care. However, a question does come to mind at this point: Is it a biblical concept, or simply the writing of an author that sounds beautiful?

Let's go no further than your own New Testament as we read, "I [Jesus] will never leave you or forsake you!" How about that for comfort in time of trouble? When you invited Him to be your Lord and Master you received a promise of His presence and power with you in all your days, good or bad, happy or sad, frustrating or wonderful! You have a Friend who will be closer than a brother. The next time you feel alone and lonely, remember this story about the footprints in the sand!

Today's Quote: *The strange thing about Jesus is that you can never get away from Him!* — Japanese student

Today's Verse: In all their distress he too was distressed, and the angel of his presence saved them. In his love and mercy he redeemed them; he lifted them up and carried them all the days of old (Isa. 63:9).

About Crusades and Crusaders

Richard the Lionhearted was king of England for ten years, but spent only about six months of that time at home. Why? Because he was so busy off crusading to rescue the Holy Land.

As a boy I liked the legend about Richard, based on a thirteenth-century romance. May I remind you of the story?

Returning from the Holy Land, Richard was captured and imprisoned by Kim Modred of Almain, or Germany. Modred's daughter Margery fell in love with him and bribed the jailer to allow him to spend his nights in her chamber. On the seventh night they were discovered.

King Modred wanted to have Richard killed there and then, but his counselors were alarmed by the idea of executing a king and preferred to arrange an "accident." The lion in the royal menagerie was to be starved for a few days and then allowed to "escape" into the captive's cell. Margery learned of the plan and begged Richard to attempt an escape but he would not hear of it.

Instead he asked her for 40 silk handkerchiefs which he then bound around his right arm. When the lion burst into his cell and leapt hungrily upon him, Richard simply thrust his hand down the lion's throat and tore his heart out!

Then, pausing only to give thanks to God, he strode up to the great hall, still bearing the warm heart in his hand. Before the astonished gaze of Modred and his court, Richard thumped the heart down on the banquet table, sprinkled salt over it, and proceeded to eat it with relish. So goes the old legend.

Some people are natural crusaders. These have a cause that is bigger than life. Occasionally they will touch home base and do some nitty-gritty work, but the cause will eventually pull them away from the humdrum.

History tells us of people like Henry Ward Beecher who stumped against slavery, and of Martin Luther King who crusaded for civil rights. There are so many causes needing crusaders today that it is a simple matter to become enchanted with a cause and become that crusader. At times it's easy to fantasize that we can take on the whole world and rip the heart out of a lion. Most of us get only a bloody arm and end up eating crow instead of heart. It boils down to this: Be careful in your crusades and keep your life in balance.

Today's Quote: *The world's moving so fast, the man who says it can't be done is interrupted by someone doing it!* — Elbert Hubbard

Today's Verse: Not that I have already attained, or am already perfected; but I press on, that I may lay hold of that for which Christ Jesus has also laid hold of me (Phil. 3:12;NKJV).

Day 27
Lessons from Geese

This fall we'll again have the pleasure of watching geese heading south for the winter. It's a beautiful sight to watch their "V" formation in action as they go by. As you observe them, you might also be interested in what science has discovered about why they fly that way.

Scientific study has learned that as each of these big birds flaps its wings an uplift or updraft is created for the bird immediately following. By flying in a V formation, the whole flock adds at least a 71 percent greater flying range than if each bird flew on its own. This was a long-term study that took place in the field as well as in a wind-tunnel under very controlled conditions.

It was also discovered that when a goose falls out of formation, it suddenly feels the drag and resistance of trying to go it alone and quickly gets back into formation to take advantage of the lifting power of the bird immediately in front. When the lead goose gets tired, he or she rotates back in the wing and another goose flies point. It's a beautiful picture of cooperation and helping each other out.

Perhaps you've also noticed that there's a lot of honking going on to encourage the leader. It's also a signal to keep up to speed.

Finally, when a goose gets sick or is wounded by a gunshot and falls out of the formation, two other geese will also fall out of formation to follow the wounded or sick goose to help and protect the wounded bird. They stay with this hurting one until the sick bird is either able to fly or until it is dead, and then they launch out on their own or with another formation to catch up with their original group.

The lessons we learn from the above are at least four:

1) Christians who share a common direction can get where they are going because they can travel on the thrust of one another.

2) If we have as much sense as a goose, we will stay in formation with those who are headed the same way we are going.

3) It pays to take turns doing the hard jobs with people at church or with geese flying south.

4) If people knew we would stand by them in the church, like geese do, they would push down our church doors to get in.

You see, all we have to do to attract people to church is demonstrate to the world that we have as much sense as a goose at our church!

Today's Quote: *If everything is coming your way, you're in the wrong lane. When everything seems to be against you, remember that the airplane takes off against the wind, not with it!* — Unknown

Today's Verse: If one part of the body suffers, all the other parts suffer with it; if one part is praised, all the other parts share its happiness. All of you, then, are Christ's body, and each one is a part of it (1 Cor. 12:26-27;TEV).

Day 28
I Need You

A country doctor told of a patient whose husband was one of those strong, quiet, taciturn men, not given to expressing his feelings. The woman was tiny and quite frail, had suffered a ruptured appendix and was rushed to the county hospital. Despite all that medicine could do she continually grew weaker. The doctor attempted to challenge her will to live by saying, "I thought you would like to try to be strong like John."

She replied, "John is so strong that he doesn't need anyone."

That night the doctor told the farmer he didn't think his wife wanted to get well. John said, "She's got to get well! Would another transfusion be of help?"

The rancher's blood proved to be the same type, so a direct transfusion was arranged. As John lay there beside his wife, his blood flowing into her veins, he said, "I'm going to make you well."

"Why?" she asked, eyes closed.

"Because I need you," he answered.

There was a pause, then her pulse quickened a bit, her eyes opened, and she slowly turned her head in his direction. "You never told me that before," she said with feeling.

The doctor, telling of this incident said, "It wasn't the transfusion, but what went with it that made the difference between life and death! Yes, the patient recovered very nicely."

Love, in order to really work, is a two-way street. We give and receive. Some of the most memorable moments of life can be the instant when someone who means much to you will whisper, "I need you."

To hear those beautiful words, as well as to say them, can make a difference in a life. The same concept holds true in the spiritual realm as well as the human. Think about this: NOT ONLY DO WE NEED GOD, BUT GOD NEEDS US! There is a constant reaching into the human realm by God. He created human beings with the ability of choice — to respond or not respond to God. That was quite a venture, quite a chance. What if man does not respond? God sent His only Son so that fallen mankind would understand about this thing called love.

Have you told someone near to you today, "I need you!" Further, have you told God today that you need Him? In order for love to be real it requires that it be reciprocal. Say it with me, "I NEED YOU!"

Today's Quote: *Wheresoever a man seeketh his own, there he falleth from love!* — Thomas A. Kempis

Today's Verse: For God so loved the world that he gave his only begotten Son, that whosoever believeth in him should not perish, but have everlasting life (John 3:16;KJV).

Day 29
Need to Be Hugged

In the fall of the year, Linda, a young woman, was traveling alone up the rugged highway from Alberta to the Yukon. Linda didn't know you don't travel to Whitehorse alone in a rundown Honda Civic, so she set off where only four-wheel drive vehicles normally venture.

The first evening she found a room in the mountains near a summit and asked for a 5:00 a.m. wake-up call so she could get an early start. She could not understand why the clerk looked surprised at that request but as she awoke to early-morning fog shrouding the mountain tops, she understood. Not wanting to look foolish, she got up and went to breakfast. Two truckers invited Linda to join them and since the place was so small, she felt obliged.

"Where are you headed?" one of the drivers asked.

"Whitehorse."

"In that little Civic? No way! This pass is dangerous in weather like this," the other chimed in.

"Well, I'm determined to try," was Linda's gusty, if not very in-formed response.

"Then I guess we're just going to have to hug you," the trucker suggested.

Linda drew back. "There's no way I'm going to let you touch me!"

"Not like that!" the truckers chuckled. "We'll put one truck in front of you and one in the rear. That way we'll get you through the mountains." All that foggy morning Linda followed the two red dots in front of her and had the reassurance of a big escort behind as they made their way safely through the mountains.[18]

Have you ever been caught in the fog of life? Visibility is almost non-existent. Then, there's not only the fog to contend with, but you're faced with a mountain pass as well. The combination can be deadly. What do you do? You need help. Hopefully at a time like that you have some mature Christian friends upon whom you can call to "hug" you through such a life-situation. Someone who can lead the way as well as someone who can follow behind with gentle encouragement.

But it doesn't stop with receiving such help. How about you? Are you willing to help someone else through the treacherous passes of life? We are to be a part of each other's life needs. Give someone a "hug" of care.

Today's Quote: *A candle loses nothing by lighting another candle!* — Anonymous

Today's Verse: Two are better than one . . . for if they fall, one will lift up his companion. But woe to him who is alone when he falls, For he has no one to help him up (Eccles. 4:9-10;NKJ).

Day 30
Lovers

Some people in a family are "gifted" lovers. They somehow know how to make all the folks around them feel the love they share, especially the love of Jesus Christ. The principles are the same in families as well as in churches or anyplace people meet.

LOVERS smile a lot. Something caring and contagious flows through them. It's inviting, warm, gentle, and kind.

LOVERS treat you as someone really special. Warmth and welcome quickly turn into genuine friendship. They like you as a wonderful person and do not hesitate to say so.

LOVERS' faces light up every time they see you. Their hugs, handshakes, and personal words make you feel totally accepted. Quickly they invite you into their conversation, group, or home. Instinctively you know that you have a place in their hearts.

LOVERS make knowing Jesus and living in Him so attractive. If coming close to Him is something like coming close to them, it has to be wonderful.

LOVERS know God. You sense that they tap into the true source of love often and regularly. The overflow of their lives show that the fruit of the Spirit is love.

LOVERS are generous with compliments from the heart, quick to see your strengths, and tender with your weaknesses.

LOVERS have flaws. Sometimes their weaknesses hurt us more than those of others from whom we expected so little.

LOVERS sometimes become victims of our rising expectations. We, and so many others, want to treat them like close friends. No one can keep up with the demands of true friendship for so many people. We can easily expect lovers to do more for us than is reasonable.

LOVERS need to be loved, too. Weddings, birthdays, anniversaries, even funerals, say something significant.

LOVERS have many who will rise up and call them blessed. And rightly so. They have blessed so many for so long that it only seems right to give them a little gratitude and appreciation in return.

LOVERS do incredible good to all within their sphere of influence. It's little wonder then that the most often repeated commandment in the New Testament is "love one another."

LOVERS are made and not born. To become a lover is a matter of decision, attitude, and commitment to become and be a lover for the rest of life.[19]

Today's Quote: *To be loved is better than to be famous.* — Eleanor Doan

Today's Verse: This is the message you heard from the beginning: We should love one another (1 John 3:11).

Notes

1. Abigail Van Buren, "Dear Abby" column, 2/14/93, adapted.
2. J. Allan Petersen, *The Myth of the Greener Grass* (Sherman, TX: Bible Believers Evangelical Assn., 1983).
3. Robert J. Strand, *Love 101* (Green Forest, AR: New Leaf Press, 1993).
4. Barry & Joyce Vissell, *Chicken Soup for the Soul* (Deerfield Beach, FL: Health Communications, Inc., 1993).
5. Richard Selzer, *Mortal Lessons,* p. 45-46.
6. Jo Ann Larsen, *Desert News,* condensed.
7. *News Leader,* Springfield, MO, 4/2/94.
8. *Moody Monthly.*
9. "News Digest," *Pentecostal Evangel,* 8/23/87.
10. Tim Kimmel, *Little House on the Freeway* (Sisters, OR: Multnomah Books, 1987).
11. Gary Smalley, *If Only He Knew* (Grand Rapids, MI: Zondervan Publishing House, 1988).
12. Josh McDowell and Norm Wakefield, *The Dad Difference* (Nashville, TN: Here's Life Publishers, 1992), p. 61.
13. John Hersey, *The Wall.*
14. Norma Copley, *The Pastor's Story File,* 7/86.
15. Chad Miller, *The Pastor's Story File,* 7/86.
16. Russell Chandler, *The Overcomers* (Old Tappan, NJ: Revell, 1978).
17. Debbi Smoot, *The Pastor's Story File,* 2/92.
18. Don Graham, Moose Jaw, Saskatchewan.
19. Chuck Mylander, *Parables, etc., 11/89, adapted.*

"Moments to Give" series

Moments for Christmas
Moments for Each Other
Moments for Fathers
Moments for Friends
Moments for Graduates
Moments for Grandparents
Moments for Mothers
Moments for Pastors
Moments for Sisters
Moments for Teachers
Moments for Teens
Moments with Angels

Available at bookstores nationwide or write
New Leaf Press, P.O. Box 726, Green Forest, AR 72638